Hippos

Patricia Kendell

Alligators Chimpanzees Dolphins Elephants
Giraffes Gorillas Grizzly Bears Hippos
Leopards Lions Orangutans Pandas Penguins
Polar Bears Rhinos Sea Otters Sharks Tigers

Published by Raintree, a division of Reed Elsevier, Inc.

Library of Congress Cataloging-in-Publication Data:

Kendell, Patricia.
  Hippos / Patricia Kendell.
    v. cm. -- (In the wild)
Includes bibliographical references (p.   ).
Contents: Where hippos live -- Baby hippos -- Looking after the calves
-- Family life -- Guarding the herd -- A watery world -- Keeping cool --
Hippo friends -- Eating -- On the move -- Threats ... -- ... and dangers
-- Helping hippos to survive.
  ISBN 0-7398-6635-4 (lib. bdg.)
  1. Hippopotamidae--Juvenile literature. [1. Hippopotamus.] I. Title.
II. Series.
  QL737.U57 K46 2003
  599.63'5--dc21
                              2002153449

Printed in Hong Kong. Bound in the United States.

07 06 05 04 03
10 9 8 7 6 5 4 3 2 1

Photograph acknowledgments:
Bruce Coleman 1 & 7 (Carol Hughes), 17 (HPH Photography),
6, 15 & 32 (Jorg & Petra Wegner); FLPA 5 (Gerard Lacz),
14 (Albert Visage), 28 (Terry Whittaker); Images of Africa Photobank
29 (David Keith Jones); K Paolillo 8, 21, 23;
OSF 4 (Rafi Ben-Shahar), 16 (Richard Packwood),
25 (Edward Parker), 19, 22 (Alan Root), 20 (Leonard Lee Rue),
12 (Steve Turner); Still Pictures 10, 18 (M & C Denis-Huot),
27 (Mark Edwards), 13, 26 (Mathieu Laboureur), 9 (Yves Lefevre), 24
(Fritz Polking).

Contents

Where Hippos Live

The great African hippopotamus lives in rivers near the grasslands in Africa.

The much smaller pygmy hippopotamus
lives in the **rainforests** of western Africa.
A hippopotamus is known as a hippo.

Baby Hippos

A baby hippo is born at the edge of a river among the **reeds.** It is called a calf. It can swim and walk very soon after it is born.

The calf will drink milk from its mother
for about 18 months.

Looking After the Calves

Mother hippos protect their calves from dangerous enemies. This hippo is roaring loudly to frighten a crocodile away.

Mother and baby stay close together.
This calf is climbing on to its mother's back,
out of the reach of crocodiles.

Family Life

One older male, a group of females, and their young live together in a **herd.** Young males live together in separate groups. Mother hippos look after one another's babies.

Guarding the Herd

The chief male in a herd will fight any
younger male who dares to enter his **territory.**

These fights are very fierce. In the end,
a very old male will have to let a younger,
stronger male take over the herd.

13

A Watery World

Hippos spend up to 14 hours a day in the water.
They can stay underwater for as long as five minutes,
closing their **nostrils** to keep the water out.

Their eyes, ears, and nose are on the top of their head so that they can lie low in the water and still see and hear.

Keeping Cool

Hippos need to stay in the water to keep cool in the hot sun. A special pink fluid oozes from their skin. This protects them from sunburn.

If the river dries up, hippos will
wallow in mud to keep cool.

Hippo Friends

Hippos will happily let birds sit on their backs. The birds catch the irritating flies that buzz around.

Under the water, hippos let fish nibble away
at the tiny plants that grow on their skin.

19

Eating

Towards evening, hippos leave the water and follow well-known paths in search of grass and other plants.

Hippos use their huge lips to cut the grass.
The places where they have eaten the grass
are known as "hippo lawns."

On the Move

The huge African hippo moves gracefully underwater by walking on the bottom of the river or lake.

Hippos can be **aggressive,** and will **charge** if they feel threatened.

Threats...

People kill hippos for meat. They sell their ivory teeth, and use hippo skin to make **cattle whips.**

Farmers plant crops where hippos live.
Then they shoot the hippos when they
eat these crops.

... and Dangers

Hippos are in danger because the places where they live are being destroyed or taken over by people.

The pygmy hippo is in the greatest danger
because much of its forest home has
already been cut down.

Helping Hippos to Survive

The shy pygmy hippo will only survive in the future if its forest home is protected.

Tourists enjoy coming to see the great African hippos in **national parks.** Here people can learn more about what hippos need to survive in the future.

Further Information

Find out more about how we can help hippos in the future.

ORGANIZATIONS TO CONTACT

World Wildlife Fund
1250 24th Street, N.W.
P.O. Box 97180
Washington, D.C. 20077-7180
http://www.wwf.org

Care for the Wild
P.O. Box 46250
Madison, WI 53744-6250
http://www.careforthewild.org

Turgwe Hippo Trust
Hippo Haven
PO Box 322
Chiredzi
Zimbabwe
http://www.savethehippos.com

BOOKS

Brust, Beth Wagner. *Hippos*. Poway, CA: Wildlife Education, Ltd., 2001.

Cole, Melissa S. *Hippos*. Farmington Hills, MI: Gale Group, 2002.

Magorian, James. *The Hippopotamus*. Lincoln, NE: Black Oak Press, 1998.

Markert, Jenny. *Hippos*. Eden Prarie, MN: The Child's World, Inc., 2001.

WEBSITES

Most young children will need adult help when visiting websites. Those listed have child-friendly pages to bookmark.

http://www.thebigzoo.com
This site has general information about hippos and video sequences of hippos in zoos getting out of the water, feeding, and yawning.

http://www.hippos.com
This site has video sequences of hippos and information about how to help them survive.

Glossary

aggressive – (ah-GRESS-ihv) ready to attack.

cattle whips – (KA-tul WIPS) whips used to guide cattle and keep them together.

charge – (charj) run very quickly towards someone or something.

herd – (hurd) a group of animals that stay together.

national parks – (NA-shu-nul parks) protected areas where animals can live safely.

nostrils – (NAH-strulz) the openings on an animal's nose that let in the air.

rainforests – (rayn-FOHR-usts) forests in hot, wet places.

reeds – (reedz) plants with tall, strong stems that grow in and near water.

territory – (TER-uh-tor-ee) the home area of an animal.

wallow – (WA-lo) to roll in the mud.

Index